Printed in the United States of America

First Printing, October 2019

CreateSpace, LLC/Amazon.com

ISBN-13: 978-1695034204

Imprint: Independently published

www.TheFinkleyExperience.com

Greetings from the Founder/Executive Director

Hi there, you future college student! I am Michael D. Finkley. I was once in your shoes; I did not know what I was doing in the process of college. I started way too late (senior year). I do not want you to be like me. I am providing you with the skills and tools I have learned over the years to assist in your college admission process. I have been employed with a nonprofit university, for- profit institutions, a technical college, and a historically, black college. Within my findings, I have put together a college workbook designed for success…**JUST FOR YOU**!

Within this workbook, your task is to track your progress throughout high school (grades 9th-12th). It is very important you keep track of your grades, courses you have taken, dates, honors, organizations, and community/volunteer hours you have earned. All of this will assist in conducting your academic **résumé** needed for the college admission process and for your future letters of recommendation. Pay close attention to the yearly checklist and tracker forms within this workbook. In addition, I urge you to visit the ***Education Commission of the States*** website to make sure you know your state's course requirements for high school graduation. I wish you nothing but the best in this endeavor in finding your way to a successful future. Let's go!

Educationally yours,

Michael D. Finkley, GCDF, M.Ed., M.S.Ed.

It's Personal

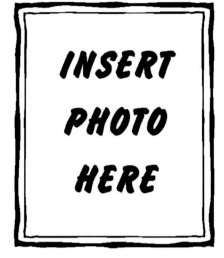

(9th Grade)

(10th Grade)

INSERT PHOTO HERE

(11th Grade)

(12th Grade)

Name:_____

Date Received: _____

Create your Personal Mission Statement

Within this statement, include all your dreams, desires, and wants. Include what you want to do for others and what you would like others to do for you. Include words from your heart and not from your brain. Be CREATIVE, Be Natural, Be YOU!

_____

_____

_____

_____

_____

_____

_____

_____

_____

_____

_____

_____

_____

_____

_____

_____

_____

_____

_____

_____

_____

_____

_____

_____

My Dream College

Directions: You might think that college is just high school continued, but it is not. College opens doors for you that high school does not. And college can change you and shape you in ways that you might not imagine.

In this activity, you will provide information that is important to you in attending college. Answer honestly and truthfully. This is an activity you cannot fail or pass. This is your opportunity to include information about your dream college.

LOCATION:

_____
_____
_____

CLUBS/ORGANIZATIONS/SPORTS:

_____
_____
_____

COST:

_____
_____
_____

MAJOR/PROGRAM OF STUDY:

_____
_____
_____

What are S.M.A.R.T. GOALS?

Goal setting is more than simply scribbling down some ideas on a piece of paper. Goals need to be complete and focused; this is where S.M.A.R.T. Goals come into the picture! S.M.A.R.T. is defined as

S- Specific: Do you know exactly what you want to accomplish with all the details?

M- Measurable: Can you calculate your progress so you can track it?

A- Attainable/Achievable: Is your goal a challenge but still possible to achieve?

R- Realistic/Relevant: Is your goal realistic and within your reach? Are you willing to commit to your goal?

T- Timely/Time Bound: Does your goal have a deadline?

S.M.A.R.T Goals are crucial to your success. Once you have a S.M.A.R.T Goal clearly defined, you need to come up with an action plan of how you are going to get there!

Finally, you need to act towards your goals. Goals will not magically happen just because you have written them down. Even if you come up with a fantastic SMART goal, nothing happens if you do not act on them.

S.M.A.R.T Goal Worksheet

Step One: Write down your goal.

_____

_____

_____

Step Two: Make your goal detailed and SPECFIC. How will you reach this goal?

_____

_____

_____

Step Three: Make your goal MEASUREABLE. To determine if your goal is measurable, ask questions such as......How much? How many? How will I know when it is accomplished?

_____

_____

_____

Step Four: Make your goal ATTAINABLE/ACHIEVABLE. Goals must achievable. The best goals require you to stretch a bit to achieve them, but they are not impossible to achieve.

_____

_____

_____

Step Five: Make your goal REALISTIC/RELEVANT. Your goal must be consistent with other goals established and fits with your immediate and long-term timelines.

_____

_____

_____

Step Six: Make your goal TIMELY/TIME-BOUND. Goals must have a clearly defined time frame including a starting date and a target date. If you do not have a time limit, then there is no urgency to start acting towards achieving your goals.

_____

_____

_____

4-Year High School Tracker

Four-Year Grade Tracker

9th Grade

Course Name	Name of Teacher	Mid-Term Grade	Final Grade

Notes of Reflection: _____

_____

_____

_____

_____

10th Grade

Course Name	Name of Teacher	Mid-Term Grade	Final Grade

Notes of Reflection: _____

_____

_____

_____

_____

11th Grade

Course Name	Name of Teacher	Mid-Term Grade	Final Grade

Notes of Reflection: _____

_____

_____

_____

_____

12th Grade

Course Name	Name of Teacher	Mid-Term Grade	Final Grade

Notes of Reflection: _____

_____

_____

_____

_____

Sports: To Do List Worksheet

Directions: Allow this worksheet to be a guide in planning your next moves in the college progress for sports. It is important to be in contact with your high school athletic director, coaches, and professional at your intended institutions of interest. This process should start 9th grade year in high school.

Athletic Director (High School)	Email Address	Office Phone Number	Cell Phone Number

Coaches (High School)	Email Address	Office Phone Number	Cell Phone Number

9th Grade Year:

Start reviewing the **National Collegiate Athletic Association (NCAA), National Association of Intercollegiate Athletics (NAIA), National Junior College Athletic Association (NJCAA), and/ or National Christian College Athletic Association (NCCAA)** eligibility requirements if wanting to pursue sports in college. You can find the specifics at the following websites: www.ncaa. org, www.naia.org, www.njcaa.org, www.thenccaa.org

**Research 10 colleges/universities you are interested in playing sports at for four (4) years

Name of Institution	Sport Interest	Athletic Director	Email Address

Other Important Notes:

_____
_____
_____
_____
_____

10th Grade Year:

Start inquiring information from your top ten colleges; you can do this by visiting the institution's website, calling via phone, or by email. ALWAYS ask for a name of the person you are talking with and jot this information in your files. You should start creating footage of self in action on the field. Work with your athletic director on this information.

Narrow your search to your TOP 5 (five) colleges/universities:

Name of Institution	Sport Interest	Athletic Director	Email Address

Other Important Notes:

_____
_____
_____
_____
_____

11th Grade Year:

Keep checking the NCAA, NAIA, NJCAA, and/or NCCAA requirements if wanting to play sports in college. Communication is key! Stay in contact with personnel on the high school and college sides.

Other Important Notes:

_____

_____

_____

_____

_____

12th Grade Year:

Discuss the NCAA, NAIA, NJCAA, and/or NCCAA requirements with your coaches and athletic director; begin composing your final footage for colleges in August of your senior year.

Other Important Notes:

_____

_____

_____

_____

_____

Freshman & Sophomore Year

Checklist
Other Helpful Documents

9th Grade Checklist

- ✓ Keep up your grades, study habits, and time management (View worksheets on study habits/time management)

- ✓ Join clubs and organizations while in high school

- ✓ Talk to your Professional School Counselor about:

  - o Education plans past high school

  - o Taking college prep courses

  - o Your high school courses reflecting your career plan

  - o Conversations about dual enrollment courses or early college programs

- ✓ Begin reviewing general college admission requirements of institutions that peak your interest

- ✓ Begin to think about how you plan to pay for college

- ✓ Start applying for scholarships for college

- ✓ Ask your Professional School Counselor about the PSAT

- ✓ Attend college/career related workshops and seminars within your school and community

- ✓ Start reviewing the **National Collegiate Athletic Association (NCAA), National Association of Intercollegiate Athletics (NAIA), National Junior College Athletic Association (NJCAA), and/ or National Christian College Athletic Association (NCCAA)** eligibility requirements if wanting to pursue sports in college. You can find the specifics at the following websites: www.ncaa. org, www.naia.org, www.njcaa.org, www.thenccaa.org

- ✓ Look for internships and employment during the summer; this looks good on your academic **résumé**

- ✓ GO TO SCHOOL AND ATTEND CLASSES; attendance is very important!

- ✓ Capitalize on your reading and writing abilities; improvements are always necessary!

- ✓ Get to know your teachers professionally; you never know when you may need a letter of recommendation in the future

- ✓ Review high school requirements for graduation by visiting the *Education Commission of the States* website: www.ecs.org

10th Grade Checklist

- ✓ At this point, you should have well over a 3.00 Grade Point Average, if not, seek assistance. Remember, you are wanting to gain admissions into a college.

- ✓ Follow all the checklist items from the 9th grade

- ✓ Meet with your Professional School Counselor as often as needed!

- ✓ Take the PSAT if you are qualified to do so; *Ask your Professional School Counselor if you qualify for a fee waiver for the PSAT*

- ✓ Start inquiring information from your top ten colleges; you can do this by visiting the institution's website, calling via phone, or by email. ALWAYS ask for a name of the person you are talking with and jot this information in your files.

- ✓ During the summer, start visiting colleges and universities of your interest

- ✓ AGAIN: SCHOLARSHIP!!!! Apply NOW!

- ✓ Start creating your academic r**ésumé and add to it as needed**

- ✓ Continue to capitalize on your reading and writing abilities!

What's My Learning Style?

**Special note: *Within developing your studying skills, you must know your learning style. I encourage you to take the VARK assessment to view if you are a visual, aural, read/write, and kinesthetic learner. Here is the website:* www.vark-learn.com/the-vark-questionnaire.

VARK Assessments Results:

Visual:_____ Aural:_____ Read/Write:_____ Kinesthetic: _____

Let's STUDY!

Study, study, study! This is one word you will hear more of when in high school. Developing awesome study skills is very important and these skills will follow you when venturing into college. A cool question to ask, how/where best do you study? Take this cool study skills assessment; I am telling you…the results may shock you!!

Question	Often	Sometimes	Rarely
1. Is there a time of day you study?			
2. Is there a place (or area) where you study?			
3. Do you try to study when you are well-rested?			
4. When beginning studying on a topic, do you quickly glance over the topic to see what it is about?			
5. Do you process information instead of just reading it?			
6. Are you focused fully when you are studying?			
7. Do you review notes from each class just for your personal understanding?			
8. Do you put notes in an outline form for organization?			
9. When studying, do you understand your notes to pass any test or quiz given?			
10. During lectures, do you pay attention and take notes?			
11. Do you think about what the teacher is saying as well as listen to what he or she is saying?			
12. Do you participate in class discussion because you prepared the night before?			
13. Do you prepare yourself for quizzes or tests?			
14. When it comes to test/assessments, do you think thoroughly for each question?			
15. When it comes to homework assignments, tests, and projects, do you write down dates, instructions, reminders, etc.?			

SCORING: OFTEN = 10 SOMETIMES = 5 RARELY = 0

A total score of **125-150**: Your study skills are solid and under control!

A total score of **99-124**: You are doing well; let's LEVEL UP!

A total score of **0-99**: There is always room for improvement; let's get to work!

What did you learn about your results?

_____

_____

_____

How are you going to improve upon your study skills?

_____

_____

_____

✓ ATTEND classes and be PREPARED for classes!

✓ Complete ALL assignments ON TIME!

✓ Take awesome notes!

✓ Review notes daily and in chunks!

✓ Time management is important; create a time plan that matches your day to day life!

✓ Stay FOCUS! You GOT this!

✓ Stay MOTIVATED!

Time Management: Do I Have Time for This?

High school is the timeframe, in your life, where you will learn about how to manage your time. By taking control of your time, you will increase your chances of success in high school and ultimately in college. The better you are at managing your time, the more time you will have to spend on your outside interests. So, the first step in improving your time management skills is figuring out how you are managing your time now.

Okay! Let's work. Within this activity, your task is to create a time log of your daily activities. Once a seven-day log is created, evaluate where you are spending most of your time and the least of your time. I am telling you; this activity will open your eyes.

	Sunday	Monday	Tuesday	Wednesday	Thursday	Friday	Saturday
Morning 12AM-11:59AM							
Afternoon 12PM-4:59PM							
Evening 5PM-7:59PM							
Night 8PM-11:59PM							

Top TEN Colleges List

College/University	Major	Admission Requirements	Cost of Attendance

College/University	Major	Admission Requirements	Cost of Attendance

College/University	Major	Admission Requirements	Cost of Attendance

College/University	Major	Admission Requirements	Cost of Attendance

College/University	Major	Admission Requirements	Cost of Attendance

College/University	Major	Admission Requirements	Cost of Attendance

College/University	Major	Admission Requirements	Cost of Attendance

College/University	Major	Admission Requirements	Cost of Attendance

College/University	Major	Admission Requirements	Cost of Attendance

College/University	Major	Admission Requirements	Cost of Attendance

Volunteer/Internship Hours Worksheet

Volunteer/Internship Opportunity	Location of Opportunity	Dates *(Month, Year)*	Number of Hours Completed

Junior & Senior Year
(This is a SERIOUS matter!)

Checklist
Other Helpful Documents

11th Grade Checklist

✓ Your GPA is over a 3.00; right? Good for you! I am very proud of you! If not, it is not too late to seek for assistance from your teachers.

✓ Because you have been working on your list of colleges, narrow your list down to five (5). From this list, check the required courses needed to be admitted versus your high school graduation requirements. Work with your Professional School Counselor on this task. Are you on target?

✓ Start visiting the colleges and universities that are on your TOP FIVE. You can do this with your high school or family. Check with your Professional School Counselor if you can miss days for college-related events.

✓ During the summer, apply for your Federal Student Aid (FSA) ID; this is how you will sign for the Free Application for Federal Student Aid (FAFSA). Here is the website: https://fsaid.ed.gov/npas/index.htm. You and your parent/guardian will need one to complete this process. If you need assistance in this matter, contact any local college and university OR your Professional School Counselor

✓ Meet with your Professional School Counselor as often as needed!

✓ Continue working on your academic résumé

✓ AGAIN: SCHOLARSHIP!!!! Apply NOW!

✓ During the summer months, look-up dates, times, and locations for the ACT and/or SAT. Proper preparation is essential.

✓ Keep checking the NCAA, NAIA, NJCAA, and/or NCCAA requirements if wanting to play sports in college.

12th Grade Checklist

✓ First of all, YAY!!! You are a SENIOR! Congrats! Second of all, what's up with that 3.00 GPA? Again, if needing assistance, reach out to your teachers NOW!

✓ Finalize your academic résumé. **You will need it when you officially apply to colleges and recommenders will need i**t for letters of recommendation—have an English Teacher edit and revise this document

✓ Reach out to your recommenders in advance if needing a letter of recommendation!

✓ You should be meeting with your Professional School Counselor more frequently than ever! Just stay connected; communication is key!

✓ College applications cost money! Ask your Professional School Counselors if you qualify for college fee waivers and ask your colleges of interest if they can waive your application fees.

✓ Do you have the credits to graduate? Check your high school requirements, PLEASE!

✓ When it comes to the college admission process, DEADLINES are important! Pay attention!

✓ If you are applying to a college for early action or early decision, check your college's deadlines. If you are not familiar with these terms, refer to *The Finkley Experience: A College Readiness Guide for First Generation Student* in Section THREE.

✓ If you have not done so, apply for your Federal Student Aid (FSA) ID; this is how you will sign for the Free Application for Federal Student Aid (FAFSA). Here is the website: https://fsaid.ed.gov/npas/index.htm. You and your parent/guardian will need one to complete this process.

✓ Complete the Free Application for Federal Student Aid (FAFSA). This opens in October 1st of every year; here is the website: https://studentaid.ed.gov/sa/fafsa. Refer to *The Finkley Experience: A College Readiness Guide for First Generation Student* in Section FOUR to see what tax information is needed.

✓ Apply for as many scholarships as you can!!! This is including local, state, and national scholarships; please see your Professional School Counselor for more information.

✓ Continue working on your college list during your fall semester; by spring, you *should* know where you will be attending the next fall.

✓ If you are not satisfied with your ACT/SAT scores, register and take these tests again.

✓ If wanting to play sports in college, discuss the NCAA, NAIA, NJCAA, and/or NCCAA requirements with your coach and athletic director; begin composing your footage August of your senior year.

✓ When your mind it set on a school, send in your enrollment, housing, and other fees to secure your space.

✓ Participate in College/Career Decision Day in the spring. This is a GREAT way to celebrate your success!

TOP Five College List

College/University	Admissions Counselor's Information	Deadlines	Additional Notes

College/University	Admissions Counselor's Information	Deadlines	Additional Notes

College/University	Admissions Counselor's Information	Deadlines	Additional Notes

College/University	Admissions Counselor's Information	Deadlines	Additional Notes

College/University	Admissions Counselor's Information	Deadlines	Additional Notes

Federal Student Aid (FSA) ID Worksheet

Student Information

Student Email Address: _____

Username:_____

Password:_____

Mobile Phone Number: _____

Answer to Challenge Questions (answers are case sensitive)

 Challenge Question/Answer 1: _____

 Challenge Question/Answer 2: _____

 Challenge Question/Answer 3: _____

 Challenge Question/Answer 4: _____

Parent/Guardian Information

Parent/Guardian Email Address: _____

Username:_____

Password:_____

Mobile Phone Number: _____

Answer to Challenge Questions (answers are case sensitive)

 Challenge Question/Answer 1: _____

 Challenge Question/Answer 2: _____

 Challenge Question/Answer 3: _____

 Challenge Question/Answer 4: _____

Free Application for Federal Student Aid (FAFSA)

Save Key: _____

Scholarships List Worksheet

Name of Scholarship	Date Received	Deadline of Scholarship

Academic Résumé Template

(First Name, Middle Initial, Last Name)

Mailing Address

City, State, Zip Code

Professional Email Address

(Standard email includes your name—first and last name)

Education

Name of High School, City, State

GPA (Grade Point Average)—if your GPA is not over a 2.50, I would not add this!

Relevant Coursework(s): Add all honors/advanced and college courses taken in high school

Anticipated Graduation Date: Month, Day, Year

ACT/SAT Scores: If you are not comfortable with your scores…DON'T PUT THEM!

Include the following sections:

- Employment (Outside of high school)
- Positions held in high school
- Volunteer experiences
- Awards
- Athletic/Sports
- Conferences

Format for these sections:

Position Held, Location/Name of Event, Month, Year

My advice to you is to be creative. This is to be a guide for you; can add or take away sections that fit your educational and scholastic standards. Please view the following example.

Academic Résumé Tips

✓ This should be a one-page document

✓ Pay careful attention to spelling, punctuation, grammar, style, and formatting

✓ Proofread your academic *résumé* carefully; have several other people proof-read your *résumé*

✓ Suggestion of fonts---Times New Roman or Arial

✓ Avoid personal pronouns and vague descriptions

✓ Use action verbs in short statements for a greater impact

✓ DO NOT repeat yourself!

✓ Write out what acronyms stand for because others may not know what they mean.

<u>Academic Résumé Sample</u>

Christopher John Doe
14xx Draw Avenue
Anywhere, Maine 03901
(555) 555-5555
chrisjdoe@gmail.com

EDUCATION

ABC Academy High School, Anywhere, Maine
GPA: 4.00
Relevant Coursework(s): Honors Courses Including: Biology II, American Government, Economics, Algebra II, & Pre-Calculus, BUS 209: Financial Accounting, COM 201: Communication Business
ACT Score: 22
Anticipated Graduation Date: June 23rd, 2020

DEF Community College, Anywhere, Maine
GPA: 3.89
Dual Enrollment Courses: BUS 209: Financial Accounting, COM 201: Communication Business

EMPLOYMENT

Sales Associate, Foot-Locker Inc., Anywhere, Maine
May 2019-Present
- Assist customers in choosing the perfect footwear for everyday usage
- Completes transactions for final sales in using company technology and software systems
- Completes stocking and other company task needed by management

EDUCATIONAL POSITION

Member, Future Business Leaders of America, *2018-Present*
President, National Technical Honor Society (NTHS), *2017-2018*
Vice President, National Technical Honor Society (NTHS), *2017-2018*

VOLUNTEER EXPERIENCES

Server/Asst. Cater, Rotary Club Annual Christmas Banquet, Anywhere, Maine, *2018*
Volunteer, Law Enforcement Luncheon, Anywhere, Maine, *2017-Present*
Volunteer, Relay for Life, Anywhere, Maine, *2016-2017*
Server/Asst. Cater, Scholarship Banquet, Anywhere, Maine, *2016-Present*

SCHOLASTIC ACCOMPLISHMENTS/AWARDS

A&B Honor Roll Award, *2016-Present*
FCCLA Recognition Award, *2018*

ATHLETIC ACHIEVEMENTS

Varsity Football, ABC Academy High School, *2017-2018*

College Recommendation Letter Template

A **College Recommendation Letter** is an endorsement of a college applicant that is written to strengthen your chances for being admitted into your dream college/university. Recommendation letters are brief, accurate statements that should highlight positive abilities and explain why the candidate will be successful and effective in their college studies.

Though friends or family might be able to sing the applicant's praises, the best letters are usually written by teachers, professional school counselors, coaches, career specialist, college/career counselors/coaches, employers, mentors, and community leaders. The individual chosen by the student should be someone that they have had a relationship with inside and/or outside the hours of school.

This letter should provide key details about the relationship between recommender and candidate and highlight the candidate's positive traits. It should include:
- *An explanation of how the recommender came to know the candidate*
- *Discuss positive talents possessed by the candidate related to success in high school*
- *Illustrates the character and competence of the candidate*

Things to Focus On:

- Highlight both the **academic *and* personal traits** of the student to show them as a real, likeable human being
- Highlight the **strengths that are relevant** to the department or university the student is applying; as the recommender, you may want to do research on the institution including the mission statement and vision
- Maintain a **confident, positive and excited tone** throughout the letter

College Recommendation Letter Sample

Dear Admissions Committee,

I am pleased to be writing this letter of recommendation on behalf of Christopher John Doe. I have had the pleasure of teaching African American Literature to Christopher during his junior and AP English his senior year here at ABC Academy High School. If it were proper for me to pick a favorite student, Christopher would be one of my top choices. He has a winning attitude full of drive and determination. He is always focused in class and has a knack for engaging the whole class in being involved.

Christopher has been at the top of his class in his four (4) year of high school. His ability to understand complex concepts, master critical thinking and comprehension has allowed him to be inducted in the school's English Honors Society his sophomore year. He is always able to manage her time beautifully and always willing to lend a hand to other students struggling with their assigned work. Christopher seems to possess the essential qualities of a born leader and able to accomplish this without an air of overconfidence or supremacy towards her peers.

English is Christopher's main academic focus, but he is also thriving in music. He has a voice of an angel. With his superb voice, he writes songs and plays the piano. I have heard him sing and play on multiple occasions and it is obvious he has an amazing attention for music comprehension. It is refreshing and confirms my belief that teachers play an important role in the educational process when you see students excel in their studies and gifts.

Any college would be excited to accept Christopher as he is an exceptional student with so much to offer. Our school was very blessed to have him as a student and I am sure your faculty will feel the same should he be accepted. I recommend FULL acceptance! I would be glad to answer any further questions you have regarding Christopher or ABC Academy High School. I can be reached via email, michael@thefinkleyexperience.com or via phone, (555) 555-5555.

Sincerely,

Michael D. Finkley, M.Ed.
English Teacher
ABC Academy High School

View the example of the scholarship criteria; answer the following questions

The Finkley Experience Scholarship
Scholarship Criteria

This one-time scholarship of $500.00 will be awarded to a graduating African American male or female high school senior who is graduating from a high school within the state of South Carolina. Applicants must:

- Have a cumulative grade point average of at least 2.50 to be eligible
- Be accepted by an accredited 2-year or 4-year college or university at the time of the scholarship award

Applicants must submit the following:

- An official high school transcript
- Documentation of involvement in extracurricular activities, volunteer and community activities, and academic awards and honors
- Documentation of FAFSA (financial aid) completed for 2019-2020 academic year
- Copy of college or university acceptance letter
- Two letters of recommendation
  (Professional School Counselor & Teacher, Advisor, or Community Leader)
- 400-word essay

Deadline: May 3, 2019

Postmark must be by/on May 3, 2019 and mailed to:

The Finkley Experience, LLC
854 Florida Blvd.
Anywhere, Maine 03901

Related Questions

Are you a graduating African American male or female high school senior?

_____

Are you graduating from a high school within the state of South Carolina?

_____

Do I have at least 2.50 GPA?

_____

Do I currently have acceptance into an accredited 2-year or 4-year college or university at the time of the scholarship award?

_____

**With any scholarship packet, ask yourself these questions. If you do not meet the qualifications, move on to the next scholarship. If you do meet the qualifications, complete the application in a timely matter. Do not be afraid to ask for assistance.

Scholarship Recommendation Letter Template

DISCLAIMER:
**Before asking for a recommender for a scholarship,
please READ the scholarship criteria in its entire!**

A **Recommendation Letter for a Scholarship** provides information concerning the candidate. This includes the qualities and achievements of the candidate which satisfies the basic criteria of the chosen scholarship. The teacher or professional school counselor will need to carefully familiarize themselves with the scholarship's requirements in order to match the letter exactly to the terms of the scholarship. Before writing their letter, the teacher or professional school counselor should talk the candidate regarding any related extra-curricular activities or any awards they may have received, and community service projects they may have been involved in while in high school. I **_highly recommend_** you submit a *r*ésumé during this process.

Things to Focus On:
- Read the necessary requirements for the scholarship criteria very carefully!
- Tailor the letter to focus on how the student demonstrates the criteria of the scholarship
- Discuss how the student not only deserves the scholarship but needs it

Scholarship Recommendation Letter Sample

Dear Scholarship Committee,

I write this letter in support of Christopher John Doe for The Finkley Experience Scholarship. I have had the pleasure of teaching African American Literature to Christopher during his junior and AP English his senior year here at ABC Academy High School. If it were proper for me to pick a favorite student, Christopher would be one of my top choices. He has a winning attitude full of drive and determination. He is always focused in class and has a knack for engaging the whole class in being involved.

Christopher has been at the top of his class in his four (4) year of high school. His ability to understand complex concepts, master critical thinking and comprehension has allowed him to be inducted in the school's English Honors Society his sophomore year. He is always able to manage her time beautifully and always willing to lend a hand to other students struggling with their assigned work. Christopher seems to possess the essential qualities of a born leader and able to accomplish this without an air of overconfidence or supremacy towards her peers.

English is Christopher's main academic focus, but he is also thriving in music. He has a voice of an angel. With his superb voice, he writes songs and plays the piano. I have heard him sing and play on multiple occasions and it is obvious he has an amazing attention for music comprehension. It is refreshing and confirms my belief that teachers play an important role in the educational process when you see students excel in their studies and gifts.

I recommend Christopher fully for this scholarship! I would be glad to answer any further questions you have regarding Christopher or ABC Academy High School. I can be reached via email, michael@ thefinkleyexperience.com or via phone, (555) 555-5555.

Sincerely,

Michael D. Finkley, M.Ed.
Professional School Counselor
ABC Academy High School

College Admissions/Scholarship Essay Writing

An essay is, *at least*, **five paragraphs**, or has many more. Make sure you follow the instructions of the prompt given (if instructions are given). Essays have the three basic building blocks: introduction, body, and conclusion.

Introduction

Begin with an attention grabber. The attention grabber you use is up to you! If the attention grabber was only a sentence or two, add one or two more sentences that will lead the reader from your opening to your thesis statement. Finish the paragraph with your thesis statement.

Body

A body paragraph is a group of connected sentences about a topic relating to the thesis statement. Because essays are composed of many body paragraphs, writing and forming good paragraphs is one of the most significant pieces of creating a well-organized and established essay.

Conclusion

A conclusion offers closure to the main points of your essay. It is the chance to influence and gives understanding. The reader should understand why they are reading your paper. An essay conclusion repeats and not rewrites your thesis statement; a strong essay conclusion contains a minimum of three sentences; a strong essay summarizes thoughts and not new ideas.

Essay Tips
- Make Sure That You Understand the Question
- Outline Your Major Points
- Write Your Introduction and Conclusion Last
- Use clear, concise and simple language throughout the essay
- State your accomplishments without coming across as if you are bragging
- Make sure your grammar and spelling are impeccable
- Read the question again and then read your essay to be certain that the essay addresses every point
- PROOFREAD!!!! EDIT!!! REVISE!!! REPEAT!!!!

Sample Essay Topics
- Your Field of Specialization and Academic Plans
- Current Events and Social Issues
- Personal Achievements
- Background and Influences
- Future Plans and Goals
- Financial Need/Hardships

Sample Writing Prompt- Scholarship

Why should you be selected for a scholarship? Please describe any academic achievements, community service activities, examples of leadership, or other personal characteristics that make you deserving of this scholarship?

Requirements: 500-700 Word Essay; 1-inch margin, 12-font size, with Times New Roman Font (You may use additional paper if needed)

**Once completed, have an English Teacher edit your work.

_____
_____
_____
_____
_____
_____
_____
_____
_____
_____
_____
_____
_____
_____
_____
_____
_____
_____
_____
_____
_____
_____
_____
_____

How to Calculate an Awards Letter

Once you have completed the college application process and the financial aid process, your institutions will present to you a college financial aid award. Based off the information you and your parent(s)/guardian(s) have completed within the FAFSA, a college financial aid award is generated. View the following example:

AID OFFERS		Fall 2015	Spring 2016	TOTAL
	Fed Direct Subsidized Loan	1,750.00	1,750.00	3,500.00
	Fed Direct Unsubsidized Loan 1	1,000.00	1,000.00	2,000.00
	Federal Pell Grant	2,888.00	2,887.00	5,775.00
	Federal Work-Study	900.00	900.00	1,800.00
	Institutional Grant	2,300.00	2,300.00	4,600.00
	Provost Scholarship	2,000.00	2,000.00	4,000.00
	Optional Parent Loan Maximum	1,620.00	1,620.00	3,240.00

TOTAL AID OFFERS $ 24,915.00

So, let's break this letter. We are going to separate the FREE money (scholarships) and the NON-FREE money (loans).

Name of Scholarship/Grant	Amount of Scholarship/Grant
Federal Pell Grant	$5,775.00
Institutional Grant	$4,600.00
Provost Scholarship	$4,000.00
YEARLY COST	$14,375.00
4-YEAR COST	**$57,500.00**

Name of Loan	Amount of Loan
Fed Direct Subsidized Loan	$3,500.00
Fed Direct Unsubsidized Loan 1	$2,000.00
Optional Parent Loan Maximum	$3,240.00
YEARLY COST	$8,740.00
4-YEAR COST	**$34,960.00**

**And this student does qualify for federal work-study in the amount of $1,800.00. Remember, federal work-study is not classified as a scholarship or loan. This is for employment purposes for students while in college. Depending on the institution, students can work on their respective campuses or within their surrounding communities.

*Always remember to be in constant communication with your institution's Office of Financial Aid.

College Financial Aid Award Letter Worksheet

Name of College/University: _____

Name of Scholarship/Grant	Amount of Scholarship/Grant
TOTAL	
YEARLY COST	

Name of Loan	Amount of Loan
TOTAL	
YEARLY COST	

Name of College/University: _____

Name of Scholarship/Grant	Amount of Scholarship/Grant
TOTAL	
YEARLY COST	

Name of Loan	Amount of Loan
TOTAL	
YEARLY COST	

Name of College/University: _____

Name of Scholarship/Grant	Amount of Scholarship/Grant
TOTAL	
YEARLY COST	

Name of Loan	Amount of Loan
TOTAL	
YEARLY COST	

Name of College/University: _____

Name of Scholarship/Grant	Amount of Scholarship/Grant
TOTAL	
YEARLY COST	

Name of Loan	Amount of Loan
TOTAL	
YEARLY COST	

Name of College/University: _____

Name of Scholarship/Grant	Amount of Scholarship/Grant
TOTAL	
YEARLY COST	

Name of Loan	Amount of Loan
TOTAL	
YEARLY COST	

Name of College/University: _____

Name of Scholarship/Grant	Amount of Scholarship/Grant
TOTAL	
YEARLY COST	

Name of Loan	Amount of Loan
TOTAL	
YEARLY COST	

Career Readiness

(Templates/Worksheets)

Composing an Email Worksheet

A formal email is typically sent to someone you don't know well or to someone who is in authority. Examples of someone who you might send a formal email to include your professor, a public official, or even a company you are doing business with. If your workplace has a formal environment, use formal emails with your boss and colleagues unless you are told to do otherwise. Many workplaces are moving towards a more casual environment and this often carries over to email communications. If you're not sure what is right for your workplace, ask!

We receive and send emails every day. An email is the best mode of communication in a particular situation and write messages that successfully convey your meaning to your intended audience. Here are some important things to remember before you send out your next email:

- Clear, concise subject line
- Proper greeting (i.e. Good morning, Good afternoon)
- Clear, concise body paragraph(s)
- Appropriate closing (i.e. Sincerely, Best regards)
- Signature (Your FIRST and LAST NAME)

***Always remember your proper nouns. A **proper noun** is a specific name for a particular person, place, or thing. Proper nouns are always capitalized in English, no matter where they fall in a sentence.*

***Suggestive Advice:** Paragraphs in email should not be indented. This is an often-ignored guideline. Your recipient is probably very busy and has many other emails fighting for attention.*

Complete the email template below:

Subject Line: _____

(Greeting): _____

Body:

_____
_____
_____
_____
_____
_____
_____
_____
_____

(Closing): _____

(Signature): _____

COVER LETTER TEMPLATE

Your Details

Name (Full Name)
Address
City, State, Zip Code
Contact Number
Email Address

Date

Employer Details

Company Name
Employer's Name
Employer's Job Title
Address
City, State, Zip Code

Dear (Employer's Name)   ,

Paragraph 1 – Reason

Example: *I recently noticed the position of Administrative Office Manager on your company's website. I feel this is the correct position for me, as my experience and education match the skills for which you are searching. I am experienced in advising, coaching and mentoring students from diverse academic, socioeconomic, and cultural backgrounds. I am strongly committed to the areas of diversity, equity, inclusion, and undergraduate admissions.*

***Always tailor section to the position you are applying for.*

Paragraph 2 – Interest

- Why are you interested in the position and the company? From the research you have conducted about the company, incorporate this information as to why you are interest; employers love to hear their information fed back to them.

Paragraph 3 – Persuasion

- Refer to your résumé and provide more details about the skills and experience that you have to offer. This is the opportunity for you to beg on yourself; not too much detail because your résumé is attached to this document.

Paragraph 4 – Action and Closing

State what you believe will occur next. Also prove that you are keen by stating that you look forward to having an interview. Sign off with 'Regards', 'Kind Regards', or 'Sincerely' followed by you signature and name.

Example: *Please find my résumé attached for your further reference. I look forward to having the opportunity to discuss my application further and am available for an interview any time. Thank you for your time and consideration of my application.*

Kind Regards,

(Sign here)

Print your name

Résumé Worksheet

First Name:_____M.I.:_____Last Name: _____

Mailing Address (City, State, Zip Code)

_____

_____

Home Phone:

_____

Cell Phone:

_____

Email Address:

_____

Education:

_____

_____

_____

Employment:

_____

_____

_____

_____

_____

_____

_____

Other sections:

_____

_____

_____

_____

_____

_____

Christopher John Doe

14xx Draw Avenue
Anywhere, Maine 03901
(555) 555-5555
chrisjdoe@gmail.com

EDUCATION

ABC Academy High School, Anywhere, Maine
GPA: 4.00
Relevant Coursework(s): Honors Courses Including: Biology II, American Government, Economics, Algebra II, & Pre-Calculus, BUS 209: Financial Accounting, COM 201: Communication Business
ACT Score: 22
Anticipated Graduation Date: June 23rd, 2020

EMPLOYMENT

Sales Associate, Foot-Locker Inc., Anywhere, Maine
May 2019-Present
- Assist customers in choosing the perfect footwear for everyday usage
- Completes transactions for final sales in using company technology and software systems
- Completes stocking and other company task needed by management

EDUCATIONAL POSITION

Member, Future Business Leaders of America, *2018-Present*
President, National Technical Honor Society (NTHS), *2017-2018*
Vice President, National Technical Honor Society (NTHS), *2017-2018*

VOLUNTEER EXPERIENCES

Server/Asst. Cater, Rotary Club Annual Christmas Banquet, Anywhere, Maine, *2018*
Volunteer, Law Enforcement Luncheon, Anywhere, Maine, *2017-Present*
Volunteer, Relay for Life, Anywhere, Maine, *2016-2017*
Server/Asst. Cater, Scholarship Banquet, Anywhere, Maine, *2016-Present*

SCHOLASTIC ACCOMPLISHMENTS/AWARDS

A&B Honor Roll Award, *2016-Present*
FCCLA Recognition Award, *2018*

ATHLETIC ACHIEVEMENTS

Varsity Football, ABC Academy High School, *2017-2018*

PROFESSIONAL REFERENCES

Definition: A professional reference is a recommendation from a person who can vouch for your qualifications for a job. A professional reference for an experienced worker is typically a former employer, a colleague, a client, a supervisor, or someone who can recommend you for employment. This does not include family and friends.

Directions: List three references who are familiar with your work and educational ethics (i.e. teachers, counselors, community leaders, employers); DO NOT include immediate family members (mom, dad, sisters, brothers, etc.)

Example:

Name: Michael D. Finkley

Position Title: Founder/Executive Director

Place of Employment/Address: The Finkley Experience, 1423 Draw Avenue, Anywhere, Maine 03901

Email Address: michael@thefinkleyexperience.com

Phone Number: (555) 555-5555

Years of Acquaintance: 4

YOUR TURN

Name: _____

Position Title: _____

Place of Employment/Address: _____

Email Address: _____

Phone Number: _____

Years of Acquaintance: _____

Name: _____

Position Title: _____

Place of Employment/Address: _____

Email Address: _____

Phone Number: _____

Years of Acquaintance: _____

Name: _____

Position Title: _____

Place of Employment/Address: _____

Email Address: _____

Phone Number: _____

Years of Acquaintance: _____

Notes

Notes

Made in the USA
Monee, IL
24 July 2021